at home with ...

The Aztecs

...in history

WAYLAND

WAYLAND

This edition published in 2014 by Wayland

Copyright © 2014 Brown Bear Books Ltd.

Wayland
Hachette Children's Books
338 Euston Road
London NW1 3BH

Wayland Australia
Level 17/207 Kent Street
Sydney, NSW 2000

All Rights Reserved.

Brown Bear Books Ltd.
First Floor
9–17 St. Albans Place
London
N1 0NX

Author: Tim Cooke
Designer: Lynne Lennon
Picture manager: Sophie Mortimer
Design manager: Keith Davis
Editorial director: Lindsey Lowe
Children's publisher: Anne O'Daly

ISBN–13: 978 0 7502 8192 8

Printed in China

Wayland is a division of Hachette Children's Books,
an Hachette UK company.
www.hachette.co.uk

Websites

Picture credits
Key: b = bottom, bgr = background, c = centre, is = insert, l = left, mtg = montage, r = right, t = top.

Front Cover: Library of Congress: main; **Shutterstock:** l; **Thinkstock:** istockphoto tr:
Interior : Alamy: National Geographic Image Collection 29r, The Art Archive 11t, 26t, Werner Forman Archive 25tr; **Art Archive:** Museo Ciudad Mexico/Gianni Dagli Orti 7tr; **Bridgeman Art Library:** Boltin Picture Library 19bl, Bonhams 13tl; **Clipart.com:** 16l, 21r; **Corbis:** National Geographic Society 1, 7cl; **Library of Congress:** 6; **Frank C. Muller:** 27br; **RHL:** 12, 18, 23t, 26bl, British Museum 19t, 29tl, Field Museum Library 21bl, Gardiner Museum 28l, Loubat Collection 11b, National Museum of Anthropology and History in Mexico City 22, National Museum of Ethnology, Osaka, 28br; **Joe Ravi:** 7bl; **Shutterstock:** 14, 15b, 17, 24, C Duschinger 15cr, Volodymyr Krasyuk 9b, Grigory Kubatyan 5b, ODM Studio 7br Studio Araminta 8, Valentyn Volkov 19br; **Thinkstock:** Dorling Kindersley RF 10, 20, 27tl, Hemera 29br, istockphoto 5t, 9tl, 9c, 13b, 15t, Photos.com 4, 23b, 25bl.

All other artworks Brown Bear Books.

Brown Bear Books has made every attempt to contact the copyright holder. If you have any information please contact licensing@brownbearbooks.co.uk

Contents

ANGRY gods, **cactus** and **warfare**
... Just the kind of world we love!

Welcome to the Aztec World

What do you know about the Aztecs?
Probably that they made human sacrifices to the gods? That they ruled a huge empire in ancient Mexico? Maybe that they invented chocolate? Correct?

Well, none of that is WRONG, but it's only PART of the story. We're going to take you behind the scenes.

Hot facts

★ **Aztec religion** was based on keeping their wide range of gods happy.

★ **The Aztecs** established a network of trade links throughout Mexico and Central America. Merchants brought luxury goods to the capital city, Tenochtitlán.

★ **In 1519** Hernán Cortés and a party of Spaniards landed in Mexico. Cortés made many alliances with the Aztecs' enemies in Mexico.

★ **At first** the Spaniards were welcomed by the Aztecs. Cortés was amazed by Tenochtitlán but horrified by the acts of human sacrifice.

✻ **HUMAN SACRIFICE!** ✻
The temple pyramid in Tenochtitlán is the main site of human sacrifice.

CENTRAL AMERICA

Empire in central Mexico

✳ DON'T LOSE YOUR HEAD! ✳
The Aztecs love the dead. They even decorate their temples with carved skulls!

- The Aztecs moved south from the deserts of what is now the southwestern United States. They settled in the Valley of Mexico in the 14th century.
- They conquered the people living there and began to build their own empire.
- The Aztec civilization only lasted from 1428 to 1521, but during that time the Aztecs rapidly expanded their power.
- The Aztec empire spread north and south of their capital, Tenochtitlán.
- The Aztecs defeated their neighbours and forced them to join the empire. That meant the Aztecs had many enemies who would help Hernán Cortés overthrow the empire.

a Day in
Tenochtitlán

If you've got a few hours to spare, our capital city has loads of attractions. Here's our guide to the must-see sights at the heart of our glorious empire.

Life at the top!
Don't climb the pyramids. They're only for priests – and their victims, of course!

A Visit to: The Great Temple

Head straight to the centre of the city. It's home to the most sacred part of the whole empire: the Templo Mayor (Great Temple).

★ **The Great Temple** is the huge stone pyramid. Only priests climb up its steep steps – and the victims they sacrifice at the top and throw back down.

★ **The serpent wall** separates the sacred area around the temple from the rest of the city.

★ **In the sacred precinct**, why not visit the ball court and see if there's a game on? You might even get to see the losers sacrificed.

★ **There are two shrines** on top of the pyramid. The one decorated with blue stripes is dedicated to Tlaloc, our rain god. The one with red stripes is for our god of war, Huitzilopochtli.

★ **Among the other temples**, look for the Palace of the Eagle Warriors. You can't mistake it. The men dressed as eagles are some of our best fighters. They are the favourites of our god Huitzilopochtli.

Fit for a King
The Aztec emperor is the most powerful person on Earth. His palace has hundreds of rooms, as well as gardens, courtyards, a birdhouse – and even a zoo. Like other important buildings, the palace is brightly painted, so you can see it from everywhere in the city.

OUT of **town:** ✔ Teotihuacan: Its pyramids are **ANCIENT**. We believe it was **built** by the **GODS**.

Island City

It's hard to believe that the whole of Tenochtitlán is built on top of the swampy southern part of Lake Texcoco! Our buildings rest on deep foundations in the soft mud. The city is joined to the edges of the lake by causeways. When the Spaniards arrived, their leader Hernán Cortés drew this map of the city.

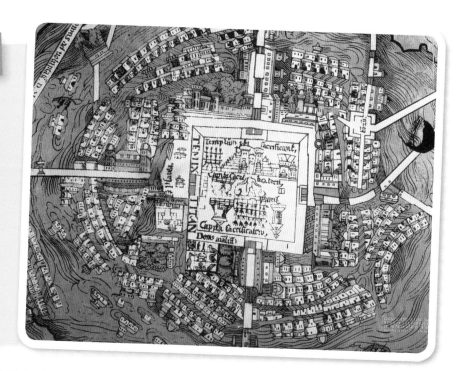

Dominant sight
Wherever we are in the city, we can see the shrines on top of the Great Temple.

OTHER PLACES TO VISIT

● You can't miss Tlatelolco, on the northern part of Lake Texcoco. It is home to the biggest market in the empire. Traders come from far to the north and south to trade goods. You can buy virtually anything there.

● Xochimilco, to the south of the city, is a floating garden. The chinampas (artificial islands) float on reed beds. They are made by filling willow frames with fertile mud from the lake. We use them as places to grow food and flowers.

Magical Eagle

When the Aztecs came to Mexico, the priests told them to look for an eagle in a catcus with a snake in its mouth. They found the sign at Lake Texcoco. It was a sign from the gods that they should build a city on the site.

Steer **CLEAR:** ✖ **AZTLAN** in the north was our **homeland** – but it's **JUST a DESERT**.

Around the EMPIRE

We Aztecs get a bad press. Everyone thinks of us as warriors and killers. In fact, we love to trade. That's why we built such a huge empire. All our neighbours join in and trade with us. We keep them fed and clothed, and they pay us taxes. Everyone's happy – why wouldn't they be?

The more gold our neighbours send us, the more jewellery we can make!

All **Roads** lead to the **Capital**

It is easy to get around. Just remember that Tenochtitlán lies at the very heart of the empire. All our roads start from the capital. They're meant for walking because we don't have any wheeled vehicles. We don't use pack animals like horses or mules either, so we have to carry everything on our backs. That means no-one moves much stuff around – unless they have lots of slaves to carry it for them.

taxing Taxation

Everyone pays taxes unless they are noble, sick or disabled. We pay taxes as tribute to the emperor. We don't have money, so we pay in goods. If a village makes pots, say, its tribute will be a number of pots. After the tribute is collected, the government shares it out to whoever needs it.

The tribute system helped us get rich enough to pay for our warriors. Some of our enemies object to 'paying tribute' – but once we defeat them and force them to join the empire, they have no choice!

Mad Meztli's Market Stall

Everything you need from throughout the empire.

★ **Maize.** All colours. Perfect for making flour for tortillas.
★ **Turquoise.** Beautiful stones from California and New Mexico – perfect for making jewellery and masks.
★ **Bird feathers.** For making headdresses and cloaks. (Please note – for nobles only.)
★ **Jaguar skins.** The best! (Again, for the elite only.)
★ **Cacao beans.** Perfect for a warming cup of chocolate or to add flavour to your favourite stews and sauces.

Mad Owner, Crazy Prices!

Jaguar skin
The jaguar represents Tezcatlipoca, god of the night sky.

Meet a Merchant

Axotl has just come back from a trip to the jungles in the south.

Q. What were you looking for?
A. Jaguar skins, quetzal feathers. You know how nobles will buy anything rare.

Q. Most Aztecs never travel far from home. What's it like?
A. I enjoy it. A lot of the people I meet are like us. Some of them don't really like being conquered by the Aztecs.

Q. You send reports to the emperor. What about?
A. A lot of us merchants act as his spies. But if I told you what I told him, I'd have to kill you!

Warriors wear jaguar skins to take on the animal's strength.

Welcome **to my** Beautiful *Home*

Don't worry too much about your home. Thanks to the hot Mexican climate, most activity happens outdoors, so we only sleep at home.

Is this your dream home?

Pyramid Street
Mexico MX-96

A BUYER'S GUIDE

- Unless you are the emperor or an important noble, your house will be just like your neighbour's.
- Go for a house with one large room with an earth floor. Don't expect a view – there are no windows, just a doorway.
- Only the rich have stone houses. Yours will have walls of adobe, or dried mud.

- Make sure there's a bathhouse outside, so you can take steam baths.
- You will need reed mats for sleeping on, chests for storing the family's goods and a few low tables.
- There should be a fire in the middle of the room (there's no chimney). The fire will have a comal on it – this clay disk is used to make the tortillas we eat at every meal.

Home DECORATION: ✔ We **LOVE** the idea of a thatched ROOF – nice and **COOL**.

Float away
We even make gardens that float in the waters of the lake.

★ **Upmarket Upstairs**

You can always tell a noble's house. It has more rooms, and it's usually built on two storeys. It is made of stone, and has much more furniture than ordinary homes. Noble families often like to build their homes around a courtyard with a pool and lovely garden. They help to keep the inside of the house cool.

★ **Homes for the Dead**

There's one thing people always find a bit weird about us Aztecs. We don't have cemeteries. When people die we like to dress them in their finest clothes and then bury them beneath the earthen floors of our homes. That way, they're still with us!

Flowers, flowers everywhere

Visitors to Tenochtitlán are always amazed at our gardens. Flowers brighten things up, and they have all kinds of medicinal properties. No wonder there are gardens everywhere you look. Our gardeners know which flowers bloom during which season of the sacred calendar. Most people have a garden surrounded by a fence of reeds. But remember – some flowers are so sacred only nobles can grow them. Don't break the law!

It's Bathtime

Our doctors tell us to bathe every day. Build a fire against a wall of your bathhouse. When the wall is hot, throw water on it to make steam. Sit in the steam until you sweat. Then use twigs to scrape the dirt off your skin. You're not just getting physically clean. You're also being pure in the eyes of the gods.

Red hot!
Make sure the fire is fierce enough to get you sweating!

✖ **DON'T** lay a stone **FLOOR** – you need to be able to **DIG** it **up** so you can BURY dead **relatives** underneath it!

Keep it in *the Family*

We Aztecs love our families. Getting married and having children is something we all look forward to. But it's not because kids are cute – it's because they will ensure our empire will survive.

Dear Agony Aunt Coaxoch,

My parents have chosen a husband for me called Ixtli. Even though he's six years older than me, he seems like a big kid. I'm only 14, but I'm sure he should be more mature. How can I get him to grow up?

Yours,

Necalli, Tenochtitlán

Dear Necalli,

Don't worry! Marriage will make Ixtli start acting like an adult. He'll be head of the household, so he will have to support you. He'll also have to pay his tribute. You'll get to look after the house, so your day will be full of cooking and weaving. Can I be invited to the wedding?

**Yours,
Agony Aunt Coaxoch**

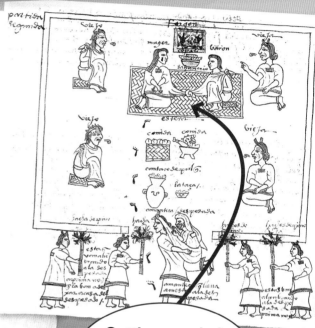

Getting married
In the middle of the wedding party, the bride's tunic is tied to the groom's cloak.

Tough Love

It can be tough being an Aztec child! You have to help with chores around the house, and there are strict rules about how you should behave. If you break the rules, your parents might hold you over a fire with chilli peppers on it. The chilli pepper smoke burns your eyes and mouth. It's a horrible punishment – but it teaches you a lesson!

Wedding fun: ✔ Choose a strong **matchmaker** – they have to **CARRY** the bride to the weddin

Chief women
Priestesses serve some of the most scary of all our war gods.

Sex **Equality**

Unlike some of our neighbours, we Aztecs are forward thinking. That's why we let women do responsible jobs, like becoming midwives and priestesses. But we have to draw the line somewhere – so not even the fiercest women can expect to become warriors.

Boys & Girls
Once they're old enough, get your kids to do jobs around the house. Girls should learn to cook and weave, plus singing and dancing. Boys should watch their dads while they work.

The cord's
the KEY

Having a baby is the most important event in an Aztec's life. Enjoy it! The birth of a baby is an excuse for a celebration that goes on for days. Here's our handy guide to make sure it all goes well.

★ **Keep the umbilical cord.** This is magic. It decides your baby's future.

★ **For a girl,** wrap the dried umbilical cord around a small piece of wood. Then bury it beneath the floor of your house. That way she'll grow up to be great at housework.

★ **For a boy,** dry out the cord and wrap it around a small wooden shield. Then give the shield to a warrior and ask him to bury it on a battlefield. That way, your son will grow up to be a great warrior.

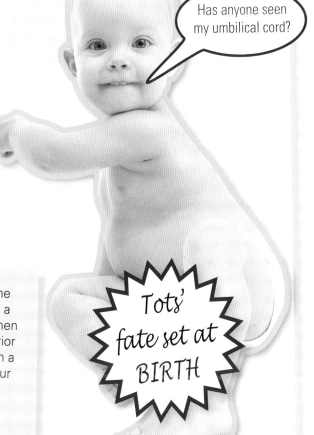

Has anyone seen my umbilical cord?

Tots' fate set at BIRTH

✓ **Ladies,** make sure you are your husband's **MAIN** wife ✖ **Don't** rush a **WEDDING** – it should last for **FIVE** days.

13

Food and Drink!

The Aztec diet is a model of healthy eating. Our enemies could do worse than follow our example. We think everyone should enjoy tomatoes, avocadoes and chocolate as much as we do!

Beware!
We drink cactus sap – but it's very alcoholic!

The Ideal Dinner Party

Don't get SPIKED!

Everyone likes to have friends around to eat. But what should we serve them?

1 **Meat is a real luxury** if you can afford it, but only important people are allowed to eat it. Farmers raise turkeys and dogs for food. Hunters catch game, such as deer and rabbits.

2 **We all love vegetables** (which is just as well, as we can't eat meat). Try serving any combination of beans, squashes, onions, tomatoes, avocadoes, sweet potatoes, potatoes, peppers and pumpkins. Stew them or roast them.

3 **Why not boil up some cactus leaves** – make sure any spikes are removed. Cactus sap also makes a tasty beer, but you're not allowed to drink it until you're at least 30!

4 **Fish and shellfish** are popular. They have to come from rivers, streams and lakes, as we are so far from the sea.

5 **To fill your guests up,** try atolli, a porridge flavoured with honey or chillies. It's one of our most common dishes.

6 **Any meal should include flat bread,** tortillas and tamales (steamed maize-leaf envelopes stuffed with a mixture of vegetables).

What's on the **menu?:** ✔ Maize, maize – and more **MAIZE** ✔ CHILLI – the **hotter** the bette[r]

Our daily bread

Everyone loves tortillas. That's why our farmers grow so much maize. The royal palace needs 20,000 tortillas a day! Tortillas are easy to make. Grind the maize to make flour, then mix the flour with water to make a dough. Pat some dough into a flat circle. Then cook on your comal (oval-shaped pottery disc) over the fire. Yum!

Family secret
Every Aztec woman has her own tortilla recipe.

Hot, hot, hot

Chilli peppers grow easily in the hot, dry Mexican climate. Some of the varieties are really hot, and they can transform a meal. Use a little dry chilli with tomatoes to make a tasty sauce. This recipe is often used after a human sacrifice. A lucky warrior who gets to eat his victim's limbs often prepares them in a stew with chilli and tomatoes.

Warning – might be hot!

Old food
Americans started eating chillies as early as 7500 B.C.E.

Expensive treat
All cacao has to be imported – so it is very pricey!

Delicious Drinks

What a treat! Try crushing the beans from the cacao tree and boiling them with water. You can add vanilla or honey to make an even more scrumptious hot chocolate. Of course, cacao is expensive – so most of us have to make do with drinking water or pulqué, a beer made from fermented cactus sap.

SALT – with **every** meal ✖ **HUMAN** sacrifice stew ✖ Cactus **stew** ✔ Hot **CHOCOLATE** ✔ Spices.

Followers of *Fashion*

We Aztecs don't wear many clothes, partly because the days are so warm. But like anywhere else, the richer you are, the better your clothes will be. And remember to follow the rules about how to dress – or you'll be in big trouble.

Get ahead
Nobles wear headdresses decorated with beautiful bird feathers.

Dress WELL for LESS!

an **Essential** wardrobe

Aztec fashion is great for people on a budget, because it doesn't change much. Young women wear what their mums wore: a *huipilli* (a sleeveless tunic) with a *cuetli* (wrap-round skirt) tied with a sash at the waist. All men wear a *maxlatl* (loincloth) and a *tilmatli* (cloak).

Only nobles are allowed footwear – but only sandals. And even nobles have to go barefoot in the temple or in the presence of the emperor.

Status cloak
The decoration of a man's tilmatli shows how wealthy he is.

Fashion **dos** and **dont's:** ✔ **Weave** your own skirt and just **WRAP** it around your waist.

A feather in your cap!

Everyone loves to wear feathers. The most fashionable come from the quetzal. Their shimmering green never goes out of style. Think of Montezuma, our last ruler. His headdress has 800 green quetzal and blue cotinga feathers.

The most luxurious garment of all is a feather poncho. They're very expensive, because they take ages to make and use hundreds of feathers.

Who's a **Noble** – and who **isn't**

Clothes are a great way of telling who is who. Slaves wear just a white loincloth; the rest of us wear white clothes. Coloured clothes are just for nobles. The richer they are, the fancier the embroidery will be. So if you see someone with gold thread in their clothes, you'll know they're very, very rich.

Colour **Crazy**

Our favourite colours for clothes are green, which reminds us of the forest, and turquoise, which reminds us of the sky. (Only the emperor is actually allowed to wear turquoise.) But the most expensive colour is a kind of red called cochineal, which is made from tiny beetles.

Dyes 4 U!

We have got the best dyes from all over the empire. Great colours to make your clothes stand out!

Blue – We've got chalk dyed with the bluest flowers. It never fades!

Green – We select the greenest plants of the forest and use them to make bright dyes.

Red – It's expensive, but it's worth it! A minimum of 70,000 cochineal beetles in every pound!

Yellow – We dry a soil called ochre, then turn it into a powder that makes a yellow like the sun!

Purple – We crush thousands of sea snails to get the ink inside them –and then we make our most popular dye!

Valuable beetle
Cochineal is so valuable that cities send bags of it to us as tribute to our emperor.

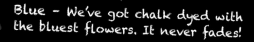

What's **your** fibre?

Most of us wear clothes that women weave from the fibres of maguey, yucca and palm plants. Only nobles are allowed to wear cotton clothes, which are much softer and cooler. Our merchants have to import cotton from the north.

Keeping up Appearances

Looking good is important for every Aztec. Follow our top tips to keep you looking your best no matter what the occasion!

Xochiquetzal's beauty Tips

Xochiquetzal is our goddess of beauty, love and fertility. She shares some of the secrets of her beauty routine.

★ **Keep it clean!** Use the roots of the *xiuhamolli* (*Saponaria americana*) plant to wash. It produces a natural soap that dissolves grease.

★ **Keep your face soft** with a mixture of yarrow and senna. Pigeon poo will help prevent freckles.

★ **To keep your breath fresh**, rub your teeth with a paste made from geranium roots, salt and chilli, or with charcoal.

★ **Some women dye their teeth** with cochineal. I don't. Who wants red teeth?

★ **Use dye** made from black clay to make your hair darker.

★ **Get rid of dandruff** with pokeberries. But be careful. The roots are poisonous!

Girls and unmarried women wear their long hair down. Married women twist their hair into two bunches and pin the two twists on top of their heads. This makes it look a little as if they have horns. It looks slightly odd, but never mind. That's how our fertility goddess, Xochiquetzal, wears her hair – and she's the example we all like to follow.

Makeover magic: ✔ Bathe every day – it's important to **keep** yourself **CLEAN!**

Chest piece
An Aztec priest wears this turquoise snake on his chest during ceremonies.

Bung on the **bling**

We have so much gold that we use it to make headbands, armbands, necklaces, bracelets, nose rings, lip rings and finger rings. Stones like turquoise and jade are just as valuable. They are ground and polished until they can be used as beads or to make masks. Also, look out for necklaces made from the red spiny oyster. When the shell is polished, it looks just like red coral.

Put a Plug In It!

Officials and nobles wear tubular earplugs. A leather earplug shows that a man is a warrior.

There are also nose plugs and lip plugs. Nobles wear gold or jade plugs in their lower lips. You have to stretch the hole in your skin over time. **No pain, no gain!**

Lip plug
Lip plugs come in all sorts of shapes.

Shiny Hair

Mix oil from avocados with axin, a cream made from squashing a type of insect (yuck!), to make a great hair conditioner.

Soak **flower petals** overnight to make **SCENTED bodywash** ✖ Grind **INSECTS** into paste to make a yellow **LIP balm**.

19

Society for *Warriors*

It is our warriors who have made the empire so big and strong. No one is more admired by the Aztecs than a brave warrior, so make sure your sons work hard at military-training school.

Get the point
Aztec warriors use bows and spear throwers to fire missiles at the enemy.

Lets have a **Fight!**

We're only here because we're good at fighting. When we arrived at Lake Texcoco, we worked as mercenaries, or paid soldiers. We fought for people who lived here – until we grew strong enough to defeat them all.

We still fight for two reasons. First, to add new people to the empire by defeating them and forcing them to pay tribute. And second, to capture prisoners to sacrifice to our gods.

How to become an emperor
You can tell how important warriors are. Each emperor has to prove his courage and bravery on the battlefield before he can start his rule.

War for **softies:** ✔ When a war is too much **trouble**, stage a **FLOWER** war with your **neighbours**

Weapons of **WAR**

A warrior usually carries a wooden spear with a blade of sharp stone. His wooden war club has stone blades set in its sides. For protection, a warrior carries a round shield made from wood, leather and cloth. His armour is made from padded cotton soaked in salt water to stiffen it.

War club
The blades in a club are made from obsidian. It's so sharp it cuts like glass.

Don't kill the **PRISONER**

It might seem odd, but our warriors try not to kill their enemies. Instead, they try to take them prisoner in as near perfect condition as possible. The gods prefer sacrifices who aren't wounded.

Hair clues
Above the age of 10, boys can't cut their hair until they have captured an enemy. If a boy still has his hair after three battles, he is officially a coward.

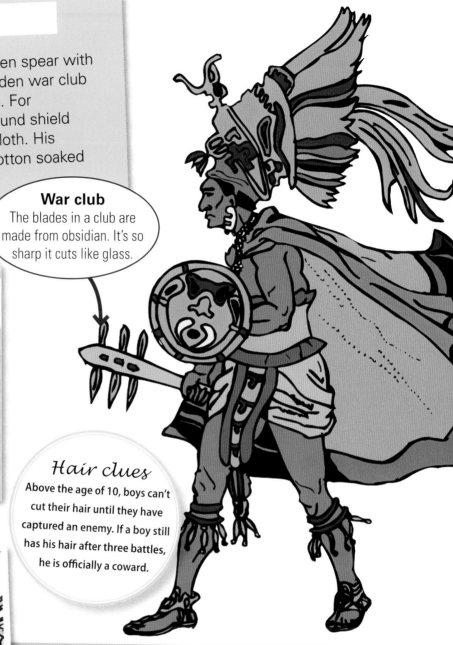

Star **WARRIORS**

Warriors who have taken at least four prisoners in battle are allowed to join one of the two warrior sects, the eagles and the jaguars. They are easy to spot. The eagle warriors wear helmets that look like birds of prey. Some even have whole suits made of bird feathers so they really stand out. The jaguar warriors wear the skins of big cats.

Only **small** armies fight ✖ Don't get **caught**. The point of the **war** is to let **BOTH** sides capture a **human SACRIFICE**!

A land of many GODS

We Aztecs worship many gods. Everything we do is meant to keep them happy. We offer them sacrifices so that the sun keeps moving across the sky and the rain falls to water our crops. Here are ten of the best!

The Top Gods

No one has time to worship all the many Aztec gods. If you keep these gods happy, you should be doing fine. Some are more helpful than others:

👍 cruel
👎 kind

👍 **Quetzalcoatl**
Shown as a 'feathered serpent', our myths say that he disappeared but will come back one day.

👎 **Huitzilpochtli**
We have to keep the god of the sun happy with constant human sacrifices.

👍 **Tlaloc**
Tlaloc is the great provider. He is the god of rain and fertility.

👍 **Coatlicue**
This goddess 'of the serpent skirt' is the mother of the moon and stars.

👎 **Tezcatlipoca**
'Smoking Mirror' is Quetzalcoatl's twin. He is the god of night, sorcery and war.

Gruesome jewels
Coatlicue's necklace is made from human hands and skulls – nice!

Sacrifice secrets:
✓ We **sacrifice ANIMALS** as well as humans. **Anything**, as long as it's **BLOOD**…

Chantico
She is the goddess of hearth fires, and lives in the fires in our homes.

 Chalchiuhtlicue
The goddess of waters wears a skirt the colour of water.

 Chicomecoatl
She is only one of the goddesses of ripe maize (there are three, because maize is so important to us).

 Mictlantecuhtli
Mictlantecuhtli rules Mictlan, the lowest level of our underworld.

 Xipe Totec
'Our flayed lord' is the god of seasons, growth and vegetation. He wears a human skin that has been flayed, or stripped from its victim.

Headwear
Chalchiuhtlicue wears a special headdress of bands of cotton.

The **Underworld**

If you die bravely on the battlefield or as a woman in childbirth, then you will go straight to the Eastern Paradise to join the sun god. If you die an ordinary death, it takes a bit longer to reach Mictlan, where the god of death lives. Your soul has to pass through nine levels of the underworld to get there. Not such a great outcome.

A **Rabbit** on the **Moon?**

One of our best-loved stories tells of how Quetzalcoatl lived on Earth. After walking a long way, he thought he would die from hunger until a rabbit offered herself as food for him. The god was so impressed by her sacrifice that he put her on the Moon. That's why we say there's an image of a rabbit on the Moon.

Feeding the Gods

In our myths, the gods sacrificed themselves to create the sun and the moon, so we do the same for them. Being sacrificed is an honour.

Sacrifices are performed on top of the Great Temple. The victim is lowered on his back onto a stone as four priests hold his arms and legs. A fifth priest slices open his chest and pulls out his heart. The heart is placed on the altar, while the body is thrown down the temple steps.

The victim's heart was still beating when the priest pulled it out of the body.

✖ Some AZTEC **nobles** sacrifice their own **BLOOD**! They **pierce** their **tongues** and **ears**! **NOT** to be recommended.

You can Count ON US

You don't build a huge empire without brains! We Aztecs know about the stars and planets, and keep track of time with two different calendars. We also have a number system and a way of keeping records.

A MESSAGE TO THE EMPIRE

To clear up any confusion about our two calendars:

The first calendar is the one farmers use to tell them when to plant the crops. It has 365 days divided into 18 months. The other calendar tells the priests when to carry out rituals. It has 260 days divided into 13 months.

Every 52 farmer's years and 73 priests' years, the two cycles end on the same day. This day might be the end of the world. We put out all our lights and fires for five whole days.

If the world doesn't end, the priests light a new flame. The flame is carried through the empire to light fires and the cycle begins again.

circular Cycle

If you're visiting Tenochtitlán, check out the huge circular stone calendar near the Great Temple. In the centre it has the face of the sun god, Tonatiuh. Around him, a series of circles tell the story of the four worlds that existed before our time. Each was destroyed. We live in the fifth world ... until it is eventually destroyed in turn.

Calendar capers: ✔ Astronomers study the **sun, MOON and stars** to keep track of the **calendar**

Reading, Writing...

Aztec scribes love to record everything. They use picture symbols known as glyphs to write down just how much tribute is paid across the empire, how much stuff a merchant sells … just about anything.

They carve on stone and write on tree bark, animal skin or cactus fibre. Since the Spaniards arrived, they even use European paper if they can get it. They make books known as codices, which are actually like long scrolls that you unroll and read from left to right.

Scribes
Trained scribes write glyphs and keep all our most important records.

The Codices
When the Spaniards arrived in the 16th century, they got our scribes to write down all sorts of information about us and our beliefs. They kept the records in big books called codices (singular, codex).

... and Arithmetic!

Counting is very useful. We use a system with a base of 20 – four hands' worth. We use dots to represent numbers 1 to 19. We have special symbols for 20 (flags), 400 (20 x 20, which we show with feathers) and 8,000 (400 x 400, which is shown by sacks of incense). That way we can record precise quantities for everything from the size of a property to the amount of tribute we receive.

We've got YOUR number!

Passing the Time!

Keeping the gods happy takes nearly all our time. Luckily, the gods are happy when we play sport or make music, so we often get a chance to enjoy ourselves.

Royal game
The emperors like to watch games of patolli.

Making a **song** and **dance**

Everyone loves to sing and dance. Music is very important to us. A religious festival wouldn't be the same without the beating of wooden drums. Drums are so important that we have two types. Which do you prefer, the horizontal drum (teponaztli) or the vertical drum (tlapanhuehuetl)? Whichever you go for, the more decorative carvings they have, the better!

Patolli

It's easy to get addicted to this board game. People have gambled away fortunes on it, or even lost their families into slavery. It's played on an X-shaped board with 52 spaces (like the number of years in one of our centuries). Two players make bets then try to win what the other player has risked. They move coloured pebbles around the board in a race. They throw dried beans on the ground. How many beans land on their ends decides how many places the player can move.

At the **ball game:** ✔ Play **anywhere**, from **Nicaragua** in the south to **ARIZONA** in the north.

Ball players
You have to be fit if you're playing for your life!

Flying high

Volador is not a pastime for people who don't like heights. It's called a dance, but it's really another ritual. In the olden times, it was said to be performed to ask the gods to end a drought.

1 Five men climb up a 30-metre (98-ft) pole that has a small platform at the top.

2 Four men wear bird wings, and have a long rope tied to their waists, which they coil up around the top of the pole. The fifth man balances on the top of the pole and plays the fife or a drum.

3 The four fliers tip backwards off the platform as it is slowly turned around. As the ropes uncoil, the birdmen spin lower and lower. If the gods are happy, they land safely after exactly 13 spins of the platform. But they get a bit dizzy!

a **game** of **life** and **death**

Our ball game, ulama, is so sacred we tell myths about it. The ball represents the sun and moon, while the court represents the earth. The most important court is near the Great Temple in Tenochtitlán.

Two teams try to hit a rubber ball through stone rings placed high on either side of the court – but without using their hands or feet. They pass the ball using their hips, elbows and knees. The stakes are high. The losing team has to give up its possessions. They might also even end up being sacrificed to the gods.

Still flying high
after all these centuries!

Play for **fun** – the game is popular with **women** and **KIDS** ✖ Try not to **LOSE** – the **penalty** is sometimes **death**!

Who does what?

There aren't many different jobs in our world. Most Aztecs are farmers, and some are priests or scribes. But what does mark us out from our neighbours is the skill of our craftsmen and women.

Sculptor

Sculptors make stone statues that show the gods and goddesses standing, sitting or kneeling. The statues are carved with lots of decoration. Even though we have no iron or bronze, sculptors use obsidian and chert tools that are hard enough to cut through any stone.

Beware, though: the stones you have to carve are often huge. There is stone dust everywhere. And a god or goddess will not be happy with a sculptor who doesn't make him or her look their very best!

Weaver

If you're an Aztec woman, you can weave. That goes without saying. You have to make all the family's clothes. But some women are truly remarkable weavers. They create complicated designs in the cloth. They are worth their weight in gold – and sometimes they even weave precious gold thread into their designs!

Backstrap loom
Weavers sit or kneel on the floor and weave on the loom in front of them.

Job advice: ✓ Aztec doctors are very important in society ✓ You need to learn all about **herbal cures**.

Face of a GOD!

the **Vanity** business

Many of our most important jobs are related to one of our favourite pastimes: making ourselves look our very best.

Heavy metal

Our goldsmiths make jewellery using the 'lost wax' method. They make a wax model and cover it with clay to make a mould. They pour molten gold into the mould through a hole. It melts the wax, and the gold sets in the shape of the mould.

Mosaic work

You need good eyesight and patience to make a mosaic like the mask of Quetzalcoatl.

Masks

You might hear older Aztecs advise you that a mask-maker can always find work. It's true. We wear masks for all kinds of occasions: for religious rituals, for festivals and for dances. Most of all, we wear them during battle. The masks our warriors wear make them look terrifying to the enemy. To be a good mask-maker you'll need to choose your material. The best masks are made of metal or of mosaics of turquoise and coral. Otherwise, you can just use clay – but be sure to paint it brightly.

Bird fanciers

The feather artist belongs to a real elite. He has to get hold of tropical bird feathers in bright colours from forests hundreds of miles away. Then he has to use the feathers to design and make spectacular feather costumes and headdresses.

Delicate work

Our nobles love to wear fine jewellery, from nose and ear plugs to necklaces of rare metals and precious stones. Every jeweller tries to make the best work he can because, like everything we do, it honours the gods.

✖ You have to get up early – **morning dew** from the fields is placed in the **nostrils** to treat colds.

Glossary

adobe Dried clay used as a building material.

barter To exchange goods for one another rather than paying a fixed price.

cacao An evergreen tropical tree whose beans are used to make chocolate.

chinampas Small 'floating' gardens built in lakes in Mesoamerica.

codex (plural: codices) An ancient hand-written book.

comal A small stone griddle for cooking over a fire.

empire A group of countries that are ruled by a single ruler, the emperor or empress.

flower war A war between limited forces that is arranged to give both sides the chance to take prisoners.

glyph A picture used as a symbol in a form of writing.

loom A frame for weaving yarn to make cloth.

mercenaries Professional soldiers who are hired to fight in war in return for money.

myth A traditional story that often involves gods or magic.

poncho A garment made from a large piece of cloth with a hole cut in the middle for the head.

pyramid A square, four-sided building that tapers to a point or a flat top.

quetzal A tropical bird with shimmering green feathers.

sacrifice Killing a person or animal, or giving up a possession, as an offering to the gods.

tamale A dish of meat or vegetables steamed inside a maize-leaf wrapper.

tortilla A thin, flat pancake made from maize flour.

tribute A payment made to a ruler as a tax and as a sign of accepting the ruler's superiority.

On the web

http://www.britishmuseum.org/explore/cultures/the_americas/aztecs_mexica.aspx
British Museum site about the rise of the Aztecs.

http://mexicolore.co.uk/aztecs/kids/
Large site about the Aztecs provided by the independent Mexicolore educational group.

http://www.primaryresources.co.uk/history/history6.htm
This site has an extensive list of links to pages about Aztec and Egyptian history.

http://www.bbc.co.uk/learningzone/clips/topics/primary/history/the_aztecs.shtml
BBC Learning Zone index of short videos about the Aztecs.

Books

Aztec (Eyewitness). Dorling Kindersley, 2011.

The Aztecs (Essential History Guides). TickTock Books, 2008.

Bingham, Jane. *The Aztec Empire* (Time Travel Guides). Raintree, 2007.

Deary, Terry. *The Angry Aztecs* (Horrible Histories). Scholastic, 2008.

Doeden, Matt. *The Aztecs: Life in Tenochtitlán* (Life in Ancient Civilizations). Millbrook Press, 2009.

Green, Jen. *Hail! Aztecs* (Hail! History). Wayland, 2010.

Guillain, Charlotte. *Aztec Warriors* (Fierce Fighters). Raintree, 2010.

MacDonald, Fiona. The Aztecs: Dress, Eat, Write and Play Just Like the Aztecs (Hands-On History). QED Publishing, 2008.

Powell, Jillian. The Aztecs (*The Gruesome Truth About*). Wayland, 2012.

Index